Observational Drawing for Students with Dyslexia

Strategies, Tips and Inspiration

Qona Rankin and Howard Riley

Jessica Kingsley Publishers
London and Philadelphia

First published in Great Britain in 2021 by Jessica Kingsley Publishers
An Hachette Company

1

Copyright © Qona Rankin and Howard Riley 2021

Front cover images source: Howard Riley and Martin Wharmby.

A CIP catalogue record for this title is available from the
British Library and the Library of Congress

ISBN 978 1 78775 142 2
eISBN 978 1 78775 143 9

Printed and bound in Great Britain by TJ Books Ltd

Jessica Kingsley Publishers' policy is to use papers that are natural, renewable and recyclable products and made from wood grown in sustainable forests. The logging and manufacturing processes are expected to conform to the environmental regulations of the country of origin.

Jessica Kingsley Publishers
Carmelite House
50 Victoria Embankment
London EC4Y 0DZ

www.jkp.com

Acknowledgements

We would like to thank Martin Wharmby for his willingness to draw to
a brief, and to Jaz and Stella for their interest and encouragement. We
also want to thank students at Curtin University, Perth, Western Australia,
Swansea College of Art and the students and alumni from the Royal
College of Art who have generously shared both work and words with us,
and without whom this book would not have been possible.

Contents

Preface

We guess that you have picked up or been given this book because, like us (the authors), you are creative and interested in art and design and also, like one of us, Qona, have dyslexia and/or dyspraxia (developmental co-ordination disorder). Qona has been working with art and design students with dyslexia and dyspraxia for the past 18 years. The motivation for our research, which in turn led to this book, actually came from our students. They told us that as well as their difficulty and slower than average ability to process words – both deciphering and recalling words – their tendency to get distracted, their confusion with numbers and their verbal retrieval speeds, they also felt that a lack of ability to draw accurately from observation had always been a difficulty. They identified drawing as an area that held them back, and even commented that people said they 'weren't good at drawing', finding it hard to draw neatly or conventionally, as Charlotte says:

> I have trouble drawing clearly. I can kind of draw to get a feeling for my (designs for) clothes. I tend to draw quite messy curvy drawings but when it comes to really clarifying, that's when I have a problem, when it comes to doing quite clear drawings.

Sadie describes how, despite being discouraged by some teachers at her school, she stuck to studying art, supported by her parents who were from an art background themselves, and went on to be a successful art student.

In Years 8 and 9 [aged 13 and 14] I was not very good at drawing and therefore, due to the curriculum's emphasis, was not considered to be very good at art. At this point, my form tutor told my mother that I was below average in the year group, mediocre at best in art. Despite the school's lack of encouragement, I did choose to study art at GCSE. There were several others like me who were not considered to be good at drawing and therefore did not continue with art. In the years since, a few of them have expressed to me how much they wish they had been good enough to continue with art. Interestingly, like me, they too were part of the Special Educational Needs group. Fortunately for me, my parents had an art background and did not listen to my form tutor and encouraged me to continue with art and I gained a place on the Foundation course at Kingston University, which started me off on my career in art and design.

We have written this book so that we can, like Sadie's parents, encourage you not to give up on drawing.

By practising techniques in this book that work for you, through dyslexia-aware art teaching, and with lots of encouragement and support from friends and family, you can learn, not just to overcome your difficulty, but to actually get really, really good at adapting and producing good drawings.

Balancing your creative strengths with proven strategies to work around your difficulties, in this case observational drawing strategies, to help with some of the processing difficulties neurodiverse thinkers have is what this whole book is about.

We will give you some simple tips and strategies that can help you improve your drawings, taken in part from some drawing workshops we've done with students. The workshops are based on some of the support strategies we use for teaching spelling and reading.

There are some simple steps and exercises around adjusting how you concentrate on looking at objects and the spaces around them, which will improve your drawings considerably.

There are many books about drawing offering techniques for improvement, but this is the first book that connects the ways dyslexic and dyspraxic people learn with tailored advice for improving drawing from observation.

In this book, you will find quotes from people who have often felt overwhelmed but are now doing really well. We've included sample drawings to illustrate different ways of looking, and illustrations of a real range of work from other artists and art students to inspire you – as well as interesting facts about dyslexia. The middle section of the book includes simple exercises to help you improve your own drawings, which you can return to and repeat to get the most benefit, so the techniques and adjustments to how you approach drawing become almost automatic for you. There are also spaces for you to jot down notes, for example if a particular art work in the book has inspired you, or for you just to doodle! You can also use these spaces to practise some of the techniques. At the end of each chapter you will find 'In a nutshell' sections — where we summarize the main ideas.

CHAPTER 1

Introduction

Imagine a world without language. Then imagine doing an activity in which the ability to set language aside becomes a distinct advantage — a strength.

Imagine a world where you could **look without language**. In this world, words don't affect what you see. When you do this activity, words wither away.

This activity takes place in a visual world. It is one in which dyslexics and non-dyslexics alike share a common ground.

We have a word for being articulate with words: **literacy**. We have a word for being articulate with numbers: **numeracy**. But there is no widely accepted word for being articulate with images, which is why we invented the word **visualcy** when we were thinking about summarizing the intention of this book! It is **visualcy**, not literacy, that becomes our most important asset when we draw.

Our book shows you how to look, and how to structure your perceptions of the world through a kind of language of drawing. The techniques and advice we offer are developed from drawing workshops we ran with students at the Royal College of Art.

Dyslexia and the creative sector

The report *Creative Graduates Creative Futures* (Ball *et al.* 2010, p.5) suggests that several years after graduation dyslexic graduates are as likely to be employed in the creative sector as their non-dyslexic counterparts.

We have written this book because we want to give you encouragement and tools to help you realize your dreams of unleashing your creativity and using it to become a fulfilled and confident individual, whether you are at school or college or are simply interested in improving your drawing.

Dyslexia: A brief history

The story of dyslexia goes back a long way,[1] it also goes hand-in-hand with some amazing individuals who have championed the cause. These champions spent their lives, first identifying dyslexia, then developing strategies to enable individuals with dyslexia to succeed at school and in the workplace, and later, putting pressure on government agencies to pass legislation ensuring that all children with dyslexia are able to access support in school.

In 2009, the UK Government commissioned research by Sir Jim Rose which defined dyslexia unequivocally as:

'...a learning difficulty that primarily affects the skills involved in accurate and fluent word reading and spelling. Characteristic features of dyslexia are difficulties in phonological awareness, verbal memory and verbal processing speed. Dyslexia occurs across the range of intellectual abilities... Co-occurring difficulties may be seen in aspects of language, motor co-ordination, mental calculation, concentration and personal organisation, but these are not, by themselves, markers of dyslexia.' (pp.9–10)

This research was hugely significant in that it stated the need to produce specialist teachers, who would work in schools and be able to provide specialist help wherever it was needed.

Research has continued since then, and the following areas have all recently been included under the umbrella term 'dyslexia'. Do you struggle with any of these? Many dyslexics do.

- short-term memory difficulties
- slower than average speed of processing words
- other sequencing problems.

Until about ten years ago, dyslexia was mostly looked at as a deficit, or a disadvantage. But then in 2011 Brock and Fernette Eide wrote a bestselling book called *The Dyslexic Advantage*, which introduced a more positive way of thinking about dyslexia and showed the advantages of being dyslexic, such as being creative and thinking creatively.

More recently, in 2015, Roderick Nicolson's *Positive Dyslexia* promoted the creative abilities of many dyslexic people, such as:

- thinking outside the box

- being a holistic thinker — which means being brilliant at seeing the whole picture rather than separate elements
- being really good at improvising with words and music
- having good three-dimensional visual-spatial skills
- being empathetic, intuitive and tenacious
- having multiple perceptual viewpoints
- making people laugh (sometimes unintentionally!).

Margaret Rooke's *Dyslexia is My Superpower (Most of the Time)* brought together over a hundred children and teenagers who talked about their dyslexic strengths (and a few challenges). Her book *Creative Successful Dyslexic* and Cheryl Isaacs' *Adult Dyslexia: Unleashing Your Limitless Power* both testify that there is absolutely no doubt that it is possible to have a successful career as a dyslexic adult.

The Bigger Picture Book of Amazing Dyslexics and the Jobs They Do, by Kate Power and Kathy Iwanczak Forsyth has many examples of some really famous dyslexics, not just in art and design but also in journalism and, rather excitingly, spying. In this book, you can read about the unique dyslexic way of thinking, and how people have coped with the processing differences that many dyslexic people have. And how their dyslexia and unique thinking have enabled them to get to the top of their professions.

As you navigate your way through secondary or high school and beyond, it is important to remember that there are many highly successful dyslexics.

We will show you a way of learning to draw that has been shown to suit dyslexic people as well as non-dyslexics.

So hold your head high, accept all the support you are offered and stand firm in the belief that after your school years, as so many of the dyslexics in the books we've just talked about show us, learning will get a whole lot easier and much more enjoyable.

Dyslexia and drawing from observation

It is generally accepted that dyslexia and dyspraxia affect the way information is processed, stored and retrieved, with problems with memory, speed of processing, time perception, organization and sequencing.

The good news is that most people with dyslexia and dyspraxia have strengths in other areas, one of which is creativity. This is now being acknowledged by a wider community; in fact, diversity of thought is becoming increasingly valued in the media and technology fields, and interestingly some architectural and design businesses look specifically to recruit people with dyslexia. Microsoft and Goldman Sachs have recently started initiatives specifically aimed at recruiting neurodiverse individuals, by altering the interview process so that it is much more inclusive.

We will return to the amazing creative potential of many dyslexic people in Chapter 3 but we are concerned here with the fact that the usual route into the creative professions, via art school, can discriminate against individuals with dyslexia and dyspraxia who find drawing from observation difficult and so may have not been able to gain Art GSCE or A-level in the UK, or College Board Advanced Placement exams known as APS in the USA.

Over the last ten years, Qona has visited a number of schools, including some special educational needs schools, and has witnessed the extraordinary and unpredictable ways many children with dyslexia and dyspraxia perceive the world (see the list of schools at the end of the book).

Many delight in channelling this different way of looking at the world into producing wonderful pieces of highly imaginative work. Indeed, you might remember when you were at primary or middle school being labelled as 'really good at art' – we all know how important being really good at something is for us. You may remember how this gained you recognition and acknowledgment from teachers, parents and, perhaps most importantly, your friends.

We have noticed, however, that towards the end of primary and middle school, many students, usually between the ages of 8 and 10, become critical of their own drawings.

If you are like some of the students we've met, you might even have tried to change your way of drawing, losing your spontaneity and confidence, and attempting to produce something that looks more of a photographic representation of what you were looking at.

This is reinforced once you get to secondary or high school where imagination is generally not seen as important as academic achievement.

Do you have memories of being disappointed by your art teachers' comments in your annual school reports as they became less favourable once you started secondary or high school?

Although GCSE, A-level and APS art curricula include themes such as abstraction, stylization, simplification, expression and imaginative interpretation, many end-of-year secondary school art exhibitions still put a heavy emphasis on figurative representation.

We have also spoken to students who have been denied the opportunity of taking GCSE Art, or the equivalent exam, at all because they have been told that their drawing is not good enough.

Here are the reports for art for two Year 9 pupils, both of whom were considered to be 'very good at art' at their primary schools. Interestingly, one of the students did do a Foundation course as she was able to take photography for A-level and got an 'A' grade!

Yet we think if we had received one of these reports we might well have given up on art. How would you feel?

'X's work is much too rushed; she has a very immature attitude, regarding it as enough simply to cover her paper with something, no matter how inaccurate or ill-considered. Her copy of a Manet was crudely drawn, the colour and tones often nowhere near matching the original. At this stage, it is doubtful that X will be able to continue with art post 16.'

'Y has a tendency to struggle in art, especially in areas of scale, proportion and drawing skills. She needs to improve her drawing techniques if she wants to continue with art for GCSE.'

We don't believe this is acceptable – although we appreciate that these teachers may simply not have understood the issues that can arise for some dyslexic or dyspraxic students around representational drawing or copying exercises, which have in recent years become such a big part of art courses.

Another purpose of this book is therefore to raise awareness that, as with writing or reading in literacy, where dyslexic students may be amazing storytellers or brilliant at analyzing a plot or character, but have issues with grammar and punctuation (details!), we believe, from our extensive experience, that something similar may be going on when they study art formally in school.

It would be great if teachers and tutors, as well as students and parents, could understand this better, and the things we can do about it.

So, armed with the knowledge and techniques in this book, maybe as well as getting better at the more traditional aspects of drawing, you can also become a self-advocate, and tell others what you've learned!

We have included many inspiring examples of dyslexic artists and their art in this book too — to show you what you can achieve and be good at.

But at the same time, we show you how to work hard to bring out your strengths, just as you may have had to with reading or spelling or fine motor skills.

We want to see creative individuals like you achieving their potential and studying creative subjects with confidence and conviction!

Chapter 1 in a nutshell

- Not drawing accurately from observation can be a hurdle

- You can get over this hurdle

- A very brief history of dyslexia

- The positive dyslexia movement and books you can read to inspire yourself

- Hard work will pay off

CHAPTER 2

Seeing into Drawing

Dyslexia-Friendly
Observational
Drawing Exercises

Introduction

In this part of the book, we show you how to look, what to notice and what to pick out in the complicated visual scene in front of you.

We then show you how to structure your perceptions in drawings.

You'll see that we don't include millions of different suggestions and techniques.

This is because these simple changes in your perceptions and approach in themselves can make a really big difference to how you draw.

And the best strategy of all is to repeat them, trying them out in different settings and with different drawing activities, in your sketchbook, on the back of envelopes or while you're sitting on the bus — or wherever — as often as you can.

That way, you will absorb these workarounds, which are more suited to your dyslexic looking and remembering thinking style, into your way of drawing. They'll become automatic.

The exercises show you how to:

- begin a drawing
- build your drawing structure
- make your drawing appear three-dimensional.

Tip: If you're working at home, find a quiet place where you won't be distracted. Maybe sit where you can look out at your street or over your garden. Or find a spot in your own room where you can arrange some of your favourite objects on a table that you can return to when you set time aside for drawing.

Try this out!

You'll see space has been left for you to draw or sketch wherever we suggest that you try and idea out. Use this to have a first try at the exercises, while the advice is fresh in your mind. Or just to experiment or doodle. Later, you might like to make further, more developed drawings in your sketchbook.

A word about equipment

Depending on your workspace limitations, you can practise the exercises in the spaces provided, or using a sketchbook or drawing board, in a seated position or at an easel. Use anything you feel comfortable with: pencil, pen, charcoal or pastel. There's only one 'rule' and it's common sense, really. Your chosen medium will dictate the size of the marks you make, and therefore the scale at which you draw and the size of your drawing! For drawings made in the spaces provided, we'd recommend a soft pencil (4B) and a plastic eraser.

Observational drawing

Most observational drawing involves looking at an object and then looking away to the drawing sheet.

This requires us to store the visual information about what we see short term in our working memory so that we can then make corresponding marks on the paper.

You probably already know that short-term and working memory problems can make it hard for you to read sentences if you're dyslexic.

Some dyslexic people talk about how the beginning of the sentence has evaporated by the time the end has been reached!

When you are drawing a representational picture, where you have to look from the subject of the picture back to the paper, you could find this difficult if you're dyslexic for similar reasons. So, working memory and processing times could be a factor affecting your drawings.

Students' experiences

Stephanie, a jewellery student drawing a skeleton, remarked:

I've noticed how quickly I lose my place, which leads to inaccuracy, so I'm starting to do this one, and as I look up I can't actually remember which rib I was looking at, so every time I'm having to countdown the neck bones and then because I'm maybe guessing which one I'm looking at this leads to inaccuracy.

Likewise, a painting student, Lu, who was drawing a still-life composition, said:

I draw one section and then I think okay, I need to keep this in proportion and then I go to another element and I completely forget about what I did before and I focus on the next element. Because I focus on the next element and I forget the first one, they are not part of the same picture. It's as if they are completely different pictures and then I remember why didn't I connect to the first element.

Jo, a ceramics student, talked about how consciously planning ahead was something she found very difficult:

> I'm trying to place everything on the page and I'm finding it very difficult. In the same way that I'm dreading starting my dissertation, I do the same with drawing. I'd rather just go into the paper and do it without consciously planning it.

Tim, an architecture student, got confused about diverging and converging lines when he was drawing in perspective.

> When I tried to do a perspective drawing I thought I was doing really well until I saw the rest of the class's drawings and their perspective seemed to go the opposite way to mine. Mine looked really right until I saw everybody else's drawings and then I realized that my drawing didn't make any sense.

So there are some common elements that dyslexic and dyspraxic students report finding difficult.

We offer some suggestions below, to help you focus your attention and keep control of your drawing.

Learning how to look: You are a TV with three channels

Like other learning processes, drawing requires practice.

Take every opportunity to make sketches of things you notice – as well as making drawings in the spaces provided in this book. Carrying a small sketchbook and pencil with you wherever you go is a good idea.

To get into the mindset of the approach we are outlining in this book, you can pretend you are a TV set, or whatever device you like to watch on, and 'tune' yourself into three different channels.

This will enable you to test or explore different aspects of what you are drawing one at a time. You'll be looking at the same scene in three different ways to see the differences: **making the familiar strange** is one of the most interesting advantages of drawing.

The three 'channels' are:

- the pattern channel
- the distance channel
- the texture channel.

There are examples of drawings that emphasize each of these three channels in the pages after the explanations, which you can look ahead to if you like.

The pattern channel

The scene you are drawing may be easier for you to translate into a two-dimensional drawing if you switch the way you are seeing it to seeing it as a flat pattern.

To do this, close one eye, and see the scene as a pattern of flat shapes.

The pattern you see can become your drawing!

Try this out now, on anything in the scene around you.

The distance channel

When we look at the world, we don't normally think about our eyes constantly adjusting their focus.

Although we're not aware of it, this is actually something that our eyes do automatically, moving between looking at objects that are close and objects that are distant all the time.

Being aware of this aspect of distance (sometimes called depth of focus) as you draw can make a big difference to how neat or 'representational' your drawing looks – how much it resembles what you see.

Before starting your drawing, hold one forefinger up at arm's length.

Focus your eyes on something in the distance, say a chair.

Notice there are now two forefingers in your vision, bigger than the chair.

Now focus on your finger, and you will notice two chairs.

Learning point: you can only focus on one thing at a time!

So as you draw, you can think about, and experiment with, using this second distance or depth channel.

Make the things that are further away look distant, not only by drawing them smaller, but by using a lighter mark, perhaps blurring their edges to indicate distance.

Try this out now. Remember, forget about all the other aspects of your drawing in the scene in front of you. Just concentrate on the distance channel – the difference between what's near and what's far.

The texture channel

The third way of changing how to look as you draw is to focus on the texture of the object or scene in front of you.

Notice how rough and smooth surfaces not only feel different, but look different.

Try this now. Experiment with making marks that show the texture differences on your drawing. A range of pencils, from 2H to 6B, will help.

Remember, the key point here is to focus on each of the channels separately at different times.

To get used to this, you should do separate drawings concentrating on each of the different channels.

Later, when you've absorbed these techniques, you might be able to consider all three channels in one drawing.

Here are some examples, with each drawing emphasizing one of the three channels of perception.

Figure 1a: Pattern

Figure 1b: Pattern

Figures 2a and b: Distance

Figures 3a and b: Texture

Drawing as a five-step process

Now you have found how to 'tune' your way of seeing the world to the three channels of perception, it's time to make more drawings.

The method we outline next is a way of helping you to draw that follows a five-step process.[2]

Each of these five steps is listed below. The technical terms (in bold) are useful when we talk about drawing.

We'll go through each step in turn, explaining each concept you'll be using in the exercises which follow:

- Step 1 Choose **format**
- Step 2 Construct **scaffolding**
- Step 3 Draw in the **negative shapes**
- Step 4 Emphasize the **T and Y junctions**
- Step 5 Draw in the tones and textures at the **contrast boundaries**

If you separate out each of these steps as you draw, it will make the composition easier to work on – in stages – and the end result will be a more representational drawing reflecting what you see.

We've again provided spaces where you can practise each step in turn, focusing on each aspect separately. Use these alongside your main drawing where you will work on the steps sequentially, building up to a finished drawing that takes in all five aspects.

Remember, the more you repeat the different steps and techniques in this part of the book, the more confident you will get!

Drawing time!

If you prefer a still-life set-up, choose objects that have some visual intrigue for you, perhaps a mix of natural forms and man-made objects.

Make sure there are gaps between the chosen objects, through which you can see the background.

And choose a position where the main source of light produces distinct highlights and shadow areas.

1. Choose format

This simply means choosing which way up you place your drawing sheet!

The two main formats are called **landscape** (a rectangle wider than its height), and **portrait** (taller than its width). **Square** is another option you could consider.

If you're using the spaces provided in the book, turn the page to the format you choose.

The **main axes** of your drawing sheet are:

- the vertical line down the middle of your sheet
- the horizontal line across the centre of the sheet
- the two diagonals of the sheet
- the Golden Section (axes which divide the sheet approximately into thirds, vertically or horizontally. Search online for fascinating examples!).

Decide how the overall composition of your objects would fit best into the rectangle (or square) of your drawing sheet by aligning the prominent features of the objects in the scene with one of these axes as a rough guideline.

This is something you should be able to do quite instinctively just by looking at what's in front of you and identifying the most important features of your still life that you'd like to be central to your composition.

Try this out for your drawing in the space below.

Below are some examples.

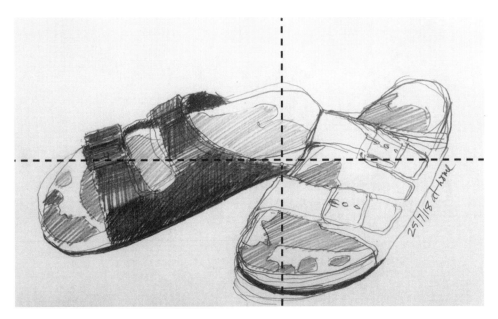

Figure 4: Landscape format, designed around the central horizontal axis

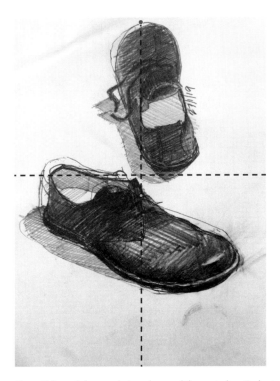

Figure 5: Portrait format, designed around the central vertical axis

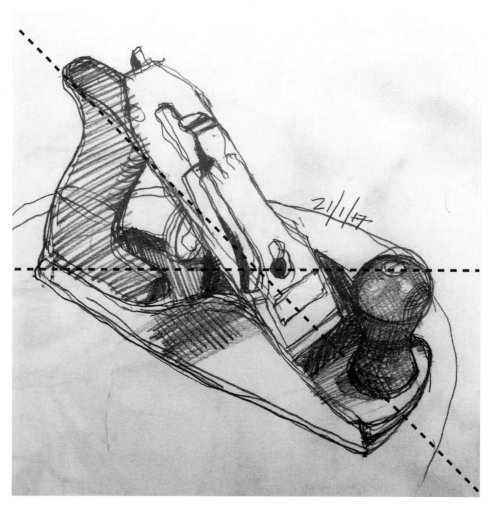

Figure 6: Square format, designed around the diagonal axis

2. Construct scaffolding

Just as the shape of a building is constructed within a structure of scaffolding, which delineates the main shapes and lines, so you can control the proportions and scale of your drawing.

Pick out the prominent points in the subject matter (if you're in a life class, use the 'N grid' which you'll already be familiar with – Nose, Nipples, Navel, kNees, kNuckles).

Draw the network of lines connecting the prominent points you've selected. This becomes a 'scaffolding' for your whole drawing.

Use the length between the first two points as a measure for the length between the other points you choose, checking back at the lines you've drawn, and what's in front of you.

Remember about **format** – try to align one of the scaffolding lines with one of the major axes of your drawing sheet.

Try this out now on your main drawing or do a draft here in this space first.

Here are some examples:

Figures 7a and b: Scaffolding of construction lines: main axes connect Nose, Nipple, Navel, kNee

You should repeat these first two steps, choosing format and constructing scaffolding lines at the beginning of every new drawing you do.

Your teacher or tutor might demonstrate these steps if you are in a class situation, or talk you through them if you ask.

3. Draw in the negative shapes

Negative spaces are the spaces in between the objects in the visual field.

So they are not the objects themselves, but the empty spaces between!

Now you have the scaffolding in place, it's time to construct the shapes of your drawing.

Don't look at the shapes of the objects in the set-up.

Close one eye and concentrate instead on drawing the shapes of **negative spaces**. We tend to see these with heightened accuracy because we have no words for the spaces in between objects, and so we are **looking without language**.

In fact, we may be using the right hemisphere of our brains, the side evolved to deal with spatial assessments, rather than our left brain, which deals with language. (For more detail of how to do this, you could consult *Drawing on the Right Side of the Brain* by Betty Edwards.)

Try this out. Your drawing may look weird at first, but in the end, letting go of your expectations about the objects and shapes can really help the drawing's accuracy.

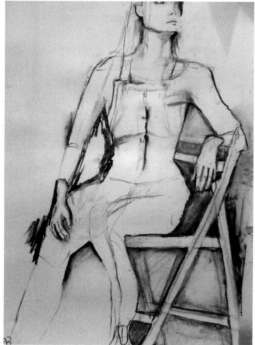

Figures 8a and b: Negative shapes

4. Emphasize the T and Y junctions

T and Y junctions are those places where edges of objects overlap background surfaces in the scene or still life you're drawing.

Close one eye. Look for those parts of the visual field where one surface overlaps two others: the edges form a 'T' or a 'Y' pattern. You can emphasize these in your drawing, or you could even make a whole drawing simply of these Ts and Ys.

Most people when drawing objects try to trace the outline. Why? Our vision has evolved to keep us safe, so we can spot anything likely to harm – or eat! – us. We are tuned to pick out the outline of the tiger, for example, not the pattern it makes with its surrounding surfaces. The tiger, however, has evolved camouflage markings, just to make life interesting! Assuming there are no tigers in the vicinity, you are now safe to study the pattern of edges made when the outline of an object overlaps the edges of surfaces in the background.

Try this out here.

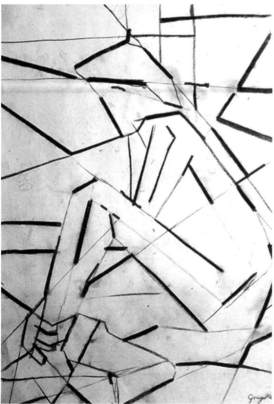

Figures 9a and b: T and Y junctions

5. Draw in the tones and textures at the contrast boundaries

The outline of each negative shape you drew earlier in step three is actually an edge, where one surface overlaps another.

Because each side of the edge is a different – contrasting – tone or texture, we can also call it a **contrast boundary**.

Using your T and Y junctions as the starting point, you can now put in the different tones and/or textures that you can see either side of your shape outline.

Notice how the contrast boundary fluctuates at the edges between the object and its background. Sometimes the object is darker than its surroundings, sometimes you'll notice the background is the darker tone.

Try this out here, if you'd like to, maybe focusing on just one part of your drawing until you feel you've got it how you like it.

There are some examples below.

Figures 10a and b: Edges: contrast boundaries between tones and textures

Step back and reflect

Once you've tried out these exercises by yourself, it's time to share and reflect on your drawings. Share them in a session of guidance from your teacher or tutor, where possible, or take some time for reflection yourself: look back over what you've drawn as you've worked through this chapter.

See which drawings you are most pleased with and which seem to work best, noting what exercises helped most.

You could ask yourself questions such as:

- Am I happy with the format I have selected?
- Which bit of the drawing am I most pleased with and why?
- Can I see more confidence in the marks I have made?

You could make a note in the space provided for your drawing of anything you feel is not quite there yet, or which you don't feel you have fully worked out.

Next time you start a drawing at school or college, read over the section in this book again, talk to a friend who's also studying drawing, or ask your teacher or tutor for advice before you start.

For example, questions you might ask include:

- Did I notice the main axis through the object I was drawing, and does it coincide with one of the main axes of the drawing box or sheet?
- Did I emphasize the contrast boundaries, the edges between tones, to make my drawing look more three dimensional?
- Did I measure between the main points on the scaffolding of the object, to make sure I got the proportions correct?

We know practice is really important if you want to get good at something. Many people believe that there are four stages to learning a new skill (see Figure 11).

If you think back to when you were learning to ride a bike, you probably started off being unconscious of what you actually needed to be doing; some people call this stage **Unconscious Incompetence**.

After a couple of goes, you might have become conscious of the fact that you needed to pedal, balance, look where you were going and hold on to the handle bars all at the same time, and you probably fell off quite bit. This stage is called **Conscious Incompetence**.

Eventually, you probably got really good at being conscious of what you needed to do and were able to do it, but you certainly couldn't do anything else, because you were concentrating so hard. This stage is called **Conscious Competence**.

Finally, you got to the **Unconscious Competence** stage, in other words you no longer used your memory to remind you of what you needed to do, you could enjoy the view, or chat to your friend, while going for a lovely bike ride, because riding a bike had become an automatic process.[3]

We believe that this stage of a skill becoming automatic can often take longer in people with dyslexia, in some areas. For example, it may have taken you longer to learn to read than some of your friends.

It's important to realize that drawing is no different and the way to get really good at it is to practise regularly.

Some people say it takes 10,000 hours to get really good, which works out at approximately 192 and a half hours a week for a whole year, which if you are good at maths you can work out is impossible!

But we reckon that if you use our strategies with regular weekly practice, even just an hour a week, you can get to the Unconscious Competence stage and still have time to go for an adventure, maybe even on your bike.

Unconscious Incompetence   Conscious Incompetence   Conscious Competence   Unconscious Competence

Figure 11: Four stages in learning a new skill

Repetition is also something that many dyslexic people find helps to make things easier, for example spelling. Perhaps you have been using the **Look, Cover, Write, Check** strategy to learn spellings. You will probably have realized that it works best if you repeat the strategy every day for a week. So remember, practice and repetition are key.

Don't give up, take pride in what you've achieved, and then...do another drawing!

Chapter 2 in a nutshell

- Practise 'changing channels'

- Repeat the five steps

- Reflect, and above all Relax and Enjoy!

CHAPTER 3

Positive Dyslexia

Drawing and Beyond

Examples of dyslexic artists' creativity

So far, this book has been about helping you to draw.

We believe that drawing nurtures your 'intelligence of seeing' (a way of seeing the world and capturing it), that can then be applied to all sorts of visual work you might go on to study. The idea for writing this book actually came from some of Qona's students at the Royal College of Art who complained that they found drawing from observation very difficult; some even said they felt they had cheated by tracing around photographs to put in their portfolios!

I had a massive problem with my degree. I actually got told by tutors that I couldn't draw, but if you're clever you can find ways round it. I always used to photograph stuff and then photocopy the photographs and then what you get is a very linear black and white flat image of what you were trying to portray. (Angela)

Another spoke about how angry and stupid she had been made to feel in a life drawing class:

Just before Christmas we had this one life drawing class. I...wasn't given any guidelines. I was asked just to draw whatever I wanted to and I was totally incapable of doing anything... I think the tears often come from the frustration and anger rather than the sadness. It's not to do with being sad it's to do with your ego being set back. I haven't been back to the drawing studio since. (Janine)

And another spoke about feeling stupid when he was talking to clients about a commission:

So I may have a client and I'm drawing them a cross section of a ring to give them the idea of what the ring might be like. I just confuse people so that can be quite embarrassing, especially if they're going to give me money for something and they just think I can't even draw it. (David)

In spite of this, all of these students have gone on to be extremely successful artists and designers. But learning to draw earlier on in their careers would have given them a lot more confidence as students, avoided heartache and saved time and money in their professional lives.

We have spent most of this book talking about drawing but this part of the book is to inspire you by showing you a selection of different types of work created by artists and designers with dyslexia and dyspraxia who have certainly not been held back by their different way of processing information and perceiving the world.

In fact, all the work here was made by people whose creative strengths have enabled them to complete postgraduate degrees at one of the top art and design institutions in the UK, the Royal College of Art, where Qona has been the dyslexia co-ordinator since 2002.

During that time, she has met many brilliant dyslexic and dyspraxic artists and designers, whose work clearly represents a myriad of ways of thinking creatively.

It seems to us that within the context of art and design the fact that a brain processes information in less systematic, predictable ways can be an advantage.[4]

We will tell you about some of the wonderfully witty and intelligent ideas that we have seen over the past few years to inspire you in your own creative interests.

Before we do that, we would like you to imagine two brains, one neurotypical and the other neurodiverse, in this case dyslexic.

Both brains are newly graduated and both are looking for jobs in the film production business. Both set off on bikes to meet friends at a cafe.

The neurotypical brain sets off, follows the map accurately, stays focused and arrives on time.

However, the neurodiverse, dyslexic brain gets distracted by the cow in the field and the crumbling bark on the oak tree, perhaps even stopping to feel its texture. The fork in the road may become an irresistible diversion; it might lead to a pond with overhanging trees you never knew existed. It's possible that the neurodiverse brain gets lost and arrives late. It is also possible that because the neurodiverse, dyslexic brain is lost they ask a stranger the way, and it turns out the stranger is also going to the same place and shows them the way. As it happens, the stranger has a film production company and by the time the two have reached the cafe, the neurodiverse, dyslexic brain has secured a six-month paid internship in the stranger's film production company.

This may all seem a bit far-fetched but would you agree that de-focused attention, an abundance of unplanned, irrational associations and apparent loss of conscious control are all features that can be associated with creative activities?

So although the neurodiverse, dyslexic brain might be described as unprofessional, and the lateness, a 'limitation' in terms of everyday life, surely we all have 'limitations' within aspects of our everyday lives, and many of them have concomitant strengths attached.

It's high time to challenge the conventional notion of 'limitation' when referring to dyslexia and other neurodiverse conditions.

The following six students were all assessed as either dyslexic and or dyspraxic. They have all become leaders in their particular areas and won prestigious prizes both in the UK and abroad, so it's not just us who rate their work.

You can decide what you think of their work and ask yourself if you would be interested in working in similar ways.

Julian Roberts is a fashion designer and has shown 12 collections at London Fashion Week and won the British Fashion Council's New Generation Award five times. In common with many dyspraxic people, Julian gets disoriented between left and right, so traditional pattern cutting was a problem for him. However, he turned this difficulty into a strength and now uses this in his design work and teaching. He calls this process subtraction cutting. He said:

I am very attuned and sensitive to numbers, but they often get in the way when sizing, cutting and constructing voluminous garment forms. I regularly confuse opposites: left, right, back, front, inside, outside... And this skill helps me re-orientate patterns in less conventional ways where dis-orientation is geometrically very useful, allowing me and my students to design unpredictable silhouettes never before constructed. My dyspraxic cutting trick is therefore a gift I gladly share with thousands of others.

Figure 12: Julian Roberts, **Unpredictable Silhouettes**

Does Julian's way of 'subtraction' working (starting with a whole form or image and then taking bits of that away) give you ideas? If so, you could write them down here:

. . . .

. . . .

. . . .

Visual perceptual difficulties are often described as 'looking at the world through the wrong end of the telescope'. The ability to see the familiar in strange ways that drawing nurtures led to this image (Figure 13) by Simon Cunningham who enjoys producing images which jolt our complacency of perception. He wrote:

I enjoy the collapse and uncertainty between inside and out... I don't want the image fixed and stable but to occupy an in-between state: dynamic and in the process of becoming, free to drift.

Figure 13: Simon Cunningham, **Mollymuddle**

Perhaps you have seen something in a magazine or online that tricks your perception in the way that Simon's photograph does. If so, you might like to jot down a reminder to yourself here:

. . . .

. . . .

. . . .

In the everyday communication of ideas, the use of metaphors can be a real strength. In a visual metaphor, one thing is represented as if it were something quite different, enabling us to form a fresh perception of its meaning.

A good example of a positive metaphor was exhibited by Bethan Mitchell at the Royal College of Art's 2018 degree show.

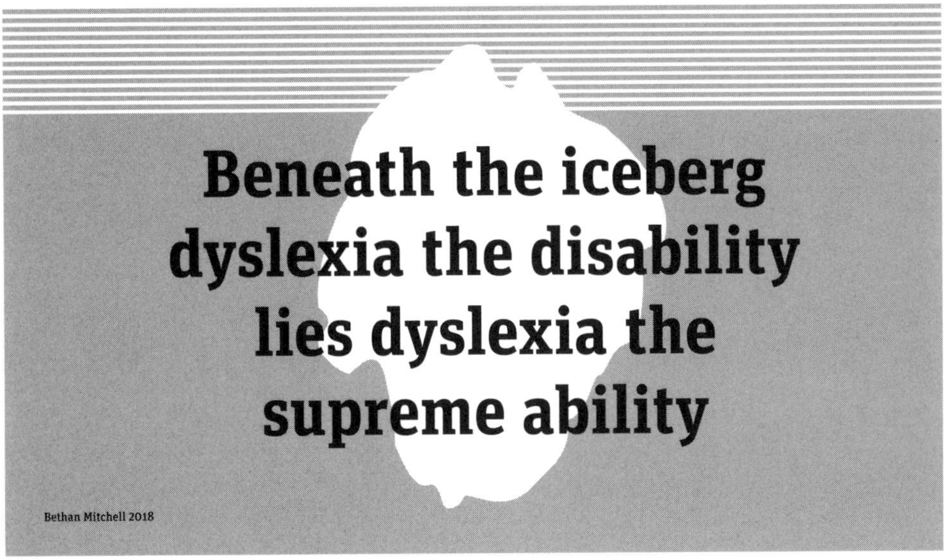

Beneath the iceberg dyslexia the disability lies dyslexia the supreme ability

Bethan Mitchell 2018

Figure 14: Bethan Mitchell, **Poster design**

What idea do you think Bethan wanted to communicate through this image? Do you think she could have been referring to the fact that the part of the iceberg that is visible is a tiny part of the whole and that the structure (hidden from view) is what gives it its strength? Or do you think she was thinking about the way icebergs are dynamic and ever changing?

There are no right or wrong answers: what is important is how the image invites you to see the familiar in a new way.

You might like to write down below what this image makes you think of, or what you like about it.

Some of our favourite ideas are produced by Henry Franks, who makes products as if they were themselves dyslexic such as the 'Confused Coat Hanger' (Figure 15) which wasn't paying attention when being told which way around it was supposed to be because it was daydreaming about whales (note the whale tail shape) and as a result has a double-hooked head.

The benefit of this is that it can hang either way round when hanging your clothes up so you don't have to turn the hanger around. Henry described how his difficulties with reading meant he spent most of his time at school drawing and making things, and how this experience has informed and inspired him in his creative practice.

I still remember vividly what it was like reading when the lines would merge, the letters would swap with the next word's letters and I would feel sea sick almost instantly. This meant that I hated reading, and spent most of my time drawing and making things. I read the physical world instead of the written world, fascinated by how things looked, worked and how they came to be the way they were. I would spend ages looking at these things and re-imagining how I would change them. Some years later from that reading experience I now channel my dyslexia into my creative practice where it allows me to make these changes and produce objects for others to look at and wonder about.

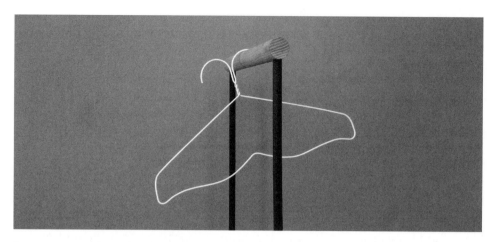

Figure 15: Henry Franks, **Confused Coat Hanger**

Do you have any ideas as to how something might be if it was dyslexic or dyspraxic? For example, what might a dyslexic map look like? Write your ideas below.

Kate MccGwire graduated from the Royal College of Art sculpture course in 2004. Figure 16 shows a work she made when she was a student and we love the irony of it — the way she has literally burnt a way through the book so that the end is visible as soon as you open the front cover. Even the title of the work, Fume, is indicative of her own difficulties and frustrations with reading at school, which she hated because she found it so hard. In particular, her reading was very slow. She recently wrote:

At the RCA I was tested for dyslexia and the results showed that I was extremely dyslexic: I scored 97 per cent in non-verbal and 3 per cent in verbal reasoning. I was 38 years old. Can you imagine how it felt to finally be able to explain the embarrassment and shame I had felt all my life? The tools and help that I got at the RCA were invaluable and I finally began to enjoy the research. Just to be able to sit in a lecture and enjoy it without trying to write illegible notes was a revelation. By recording the lecture and writing my notes later I could actually process the information. It liberated me from my insecurities and gave me the techniques I needed to learn things my way.

Kate is now a successful internationally renowned sculptor.

Figure 16: Kate MccGwire, **Fume**

Could you make a book into a piece of art? If so what might you do to it?

You can write any ideas below before you forget them.

Keeping the viewpoint constant and still is something many dyslexic people say they find hard to do.

Mirry Stolzenberg, who graduated in 2016, has used this to her advantage in creating fascinating illustrations, which enable us to experience what it is like to have multiple viewpoints simultaneously.

She uses her illustrations to take the reader on a journey around the internal life of an apartment building. With each turn of the page the reader wanders deeper and deeper into the fabric of its rooms, walls and passages – and simultaneously deeper into the (otherwise hidden) lives of its inhabitants. Like Julian and Kate, Mirry didn't discover her dyslexia until she was a postgraduate student. She used the support on offer and, having previously avoided writing as much as possible, she achieved a distinction for her dissertation. She said that getting a distinction enabled her to:

...become much more receptive and confident; it was like a roof being lifted off the sky. I was so relieved to discover I wasn't of low intelligence. Getting a distinction has enabled me to reframe my world and connect to a part of myself I didn't know existed.

Figure 17: Mirry Stolzenberg, **Market Square**

You could try doing a drawing from different viewpoints; for example, if you think of your classroom or studio, every pupil will have a slightly different view of the teacher and the teacher will also have a very different view of the class.

If this is an idea that you might like to explore then write down your ideas here before you forget them:

. . . .

. . . .

. . . .

Neuroscience has compared what happens in a task such as reading, between a neurotypical and a dyslexic brain.

The resulting FMRI scans (as reported by David Sousa in his 2007 book, *How the Special Needs Brain Learns*) reveal that reading is slower in the dyslexic brain because the messages don't take the most direct route to the part of the brain they need to get to.

This means that instead of reading 240 words a minute, the dyslexic brain may read 150 words a minute, but at the same time it could be making all sorts of fascinating connections and links through dipping into its other processing centres.

The dyslexic brain cycling off to the cafe via the slower route may in fact reveal all sorts of creative opportunities.

As we said at the start of the book, the time is right to get rid of the 'deficit model' which sees dyslexia as a disadvantage, and to embrace the much more positive approach that is emerging.

We believe, along with many others, that dyslexia enables different ways of processing information – an ability to think outside the box.

Sadly, this can often become a weakness or disability within the context of our education system with its heavy emphasis on linear learning and rewarding individuals with the ability to memorize facts and regurgitate them during examinations.

We have always preferred to emphasize the individual strengths possessed by many dyslexic and neurodiverse people. It is very likely that this ability to think more like a grasshopper – jumping around unpredictably – than an inchworm – linear and predictable in its movements – has given an edge to their creativity and enabled them to come up with original and unpredictable solutions to problems, some of which you have seen in the illustrations in this part of the book.

Imagine being a very good runner but a hopeless jumper and entering a hurdle race: if the aim is to get over the hurdles in as imaginative a way as possible, you **could** win the race; however, if you are forced to stick to the rules, you might well come last.

Inspired by the notion of the positive dyslexia movement, Qona recently ran a project where she introduced her postgraduate students to a group of children attending a local special needs school. She wanted to give the students the opportunity to contribute to the positive dyslexia movement by inspiring children with dyslexia and other neurodiverse conditions.

The aim was to show the students themselves, and their teachers and classmates, how their particular strengths fed into their creative expertise and how this could lead, in the long run, to professional opportunities. In this way, we could motivate children to explore their own creativity and at the same time educate the children's parents about the various professional pathways within art and design, so that they could encourage their children's different ways of thinking.

One resulting idea was that we might design a website, to be called *Dyslexic Superpowers*. It would be a visual and very interactive mindmap that emphasizes the strengths of dyslexics' minds.

So now you have learned how people with directional confusion, visual, perceptual, processing difficulties, difficulty with words (reading and writing), difficulties with numbers, and a tendency to get easily distracted have used these ways of thinking to achieve great things in their creative fields.

You have also learned that by practising techniques in this book that work for you, through dyslexia-aware art teaching, and with lots of encouragement and support from friends and family, you can learn, not just to overcome your difficulty, but to actually get really, really good at adapting and producing good drawings.

This optimistic view that balances the creative strengths and offers proven strategies – in this case observational drawing strategies – to help with some of the processing difficulties neurodiverse thinkers have, is what underpins this book.

Finally, we hope you now believe that it is never too late to re-create yourself as a confident, independent, successful individual, using your considerable strengths to have an exciting and fulfilling career.

A note on a new way of seeing 'seeing': Visualcy!

Nobody can remember the first sound or the first mark they made, but someone in your family will tell you what your first word was, and may even have kept an example of one of your earliest doodles.

It would not be until later that you would have been taught how to read and write (possibly your name). Communication through sound and mark-making come naturally.

However, reading and writing need to be taught. We need to learn that arbitrary marks we call the alphabet hold specific meanings within our culture.

In a similar way, you can make a drawing of an object that for you represents the object. However, for someone else it may just look like some unidentifiable shapes on paper.

In the same way that we have agreed codes for writing and reading, mastery of which we term **literacy**, similarly we have conventions for drawing requiring the mastery of conventions of visual communication. We called this **visualcy** earlier in the book.

The majority of us develop abilities in language, music and art naturally from birth. Some babies as young as two months can start to mimic sounds and produce some burbles sounding similar to vowels. Give a baby of around four months a rattle or bells and they will appear to enjoy controlling the rhythms. Being able to hold a pencil or crayon comes a little later in the development stage, at around a year. Once a baby starts to scribble, the marks quickly develop and take on meaning, as they have done throughout history.

Members of our species were making drawings in the caves of northern Spain at least 41,000 years ago.

We were certainly drawing long before we were writing: a date of around 5000 years ago in the Middle East is generally agreed for the first writing – codified marks on a surface to represent speech.

In fact, our ability to draw gave birth to the very notion of written language: the recognition that a drawn mark **resembles** some aspect of the real object to which it refers allows the possibility of experimenting with the act of drawing marks itself.

Through many hours of practice, a further insight arises from the recognition of depiction (drawing) as depiction (representation): that meaning might be attributed to a drawn mark which does **not** resemble the object to which it refers. In other words, a sign which is not **iconic**, but quite arbitrary – a **symbol** (Figure 18).

Figure 18: Three types of sign:
- **Iconic**: the silhouette image **resembles** children.
- **Index**: the location of the sign **is caused by** the location of the school.
- **Symbol**: the red triangle **is conventionally agreed** to signify danger; the words, too, are conventionally agreed.

This leads to the concept of a conventional code, and opens up the possibilities of languages, where quite arbitrary sounds, gestures or marks are assigned specific meanings with the agreement of the community. This is the overwhelming importance that the making of images has in human cultural history.

The three 'R's revisited

Our education system still doesn't fully recognize the importance of nurturing drawing.

The three **R**s – **R**eading, w**R**iting and a**R**ithmetic – are generally agreed to stand for the important educational priorities of literacy and numeracy. However, w**R**iting itself is evidence of another skill of educational value: our ability to inscribe marks on a surface so as to make meaningful representations of our experiences visible to others.

It may be argued that the centrality of w**R**iting within the familiar 'three Rs' has overshadowed the cultural importance of that other skill for which there is no name.

We have suggested **visualcy** because it refers to our capacity for drawing. Professor of Drawing, Deanna Petherbridge (1991, p.7) has said that: 'Drawing is the primal means of symbolic communication, which predates and embraces writing, and functions as a tool of conceptualisation parallel with language.'

And in our book we've unpacked for you some of the fundamental skills you need to master this capacity to draw.

In a world that depends more and more on global communication through visual media, those with a high degree of what we are calling visualcy or visual sense will be valued more and more.

This book will help you to improve and enjoy your drawing, and inspire you to be your most free and creative self, on the way to finding your place in the world of visual communication.

Chapter 3 in a nutshell

- Dyslexic/dyspraxic processing strengths

- Some examples of art works produced by dyslexics using these strengths

- You are the thinkers of the future

Endnotes

1. The first scientists to recognize the condition we now term 'dyslexia', back in 1877, called it 'word blindness'. This was almost 150 years ago when Adolf Kussmaul, a German physician, first diagnosed it. It wasn't until ten years later that Rudolf Berlin, the German ophthalmologist, came up with the word **dyslexia**. The first academic paper on the subject, 'A case of congenital word blindness' by Pringle Morgan was published in 1896 by the *British Medical Journal*. Then in 1917 opthalmologist James Hinshelwood published his book *Congenital Word Blindness*.

At that time, dyslexia was seen as hereditary and a visual problem, and for many years experts believed that the main cause of dyslexia was difficulties with visual processing. By the 1970s, cognitive psychologists (who are people who are interested in how the brain perceives, thinks, learns and remembers and how that can affect behaviour) became very interested in the process of reading and dyslexia. In 1979, Frank Vellutino published an important book called *Dyslexia: Theory and Research* in which he argued that, contrary to the view that dyslexia was some kind of visual perceptual problem, the actual problem was in how visual information is coded verbally. This encouraged many more researchers to develop theories, which in turn enabled teachers to develop ways of teaching students who learned a little bit differently. If you are interested in finding out more about this there is a very clear timeline on the Oxford University website, which also includes reference to sources mentioned above: https://dyslexiahistory.web.ox.ac.uk/home. There is also an excellent small book that was published in 2019 called *Dyslexia: A Very Short Introduction* by Margaret Snowling.

2. While we are introducing concepts well known to most competent teachers of drawing, the exercises described in this book are based on an **inclusive** teaching strategy designed to help you to build on your learning through repetitive procedures. We have adapted these repetitive procedures from well-accepted writers and educationalists such as Sherrie Nist and Kate Kirby (1986), Sherrie Nist and Donna Mealey (1991), Tilly Mortimore (2003) and Gavin Reid (2016).

3. Angela Fawcett (2001) and Roderick Nicolson (2015) share a theory they call 'automatization deficit'. 'Automatic' refers to processing that does not require attention, as in the case of the final bike drawing in Figure 11, 'Unconscious Competence'. Both Nicholson and Fawcett have argued that dyslexic children often have tremendous difficulty making skills automatic, thus they could be said to suffer from 'automatization deficit'.

4. In 2012, James Redford made a film about his son Dylan's dyslexia called *The Big Picture*. The title acknowledged the strength many dyslexic people have in being able to see the whole picture, and even beyond it. In the film, Dylan speaks about how difficult it can be to work sequentially, and how he has strategies that can help him. Entrepreneur Richard Branson, who appears in the film, attributes his own professional success partially to being a very good 'wholist thinker' — although he does not use this term — and also to being able to employ a team who are excellent at working out the details that enable him to achieve his goals. The academic John Stein gave a talk some years ago called *Wobbles, Warbles and Fish*, referring to why many dyslexic people have difficulty reading accurately and at the same speed as neurotypical people. Stein used the phrases 'visual motor sensitivity' and 'impaired binocular vision'. He went on to explain the role of Parvo and Magno cells: the job of Parvo cells is to be really efficient at peripheral vision and so enable you to see the whole page; Magno cells are particularly good at focusing on individual words. As you can imagine, you need both when reading, but apparently many dyslexics rely mainly on Parvo cells when reading, so you get the picture generally, but not necessarily the minute details. When Qona attended Stein's talk, in her head she substituted the verb 'drawing', for 'reading' and thought that using Parvo cells might make you good at drawing the whole picture, but that you would need the Magno cells to be fully operational in order to draw the details accurately.

List of primary schools visited by Qona Rankin

Abingdon House School
www.abingdonhouseschool.co.uk

Anstruther House
https://mpschool.co.uk/autism-provision

Brent Knoll
www.brentknoll.lewisham.sch.uk

Fairley House School
www.fairleyhouse.org.uk

Granta School
www.granta.cambs.sch.uk/website

Marlborough Primary School
https://mpschool.co.uk

Paddock School
www.paddock.wandsworth.sch.uk

St Marylebone Bridge School
www.stmarylebonebridgeschool.com

Swan Centre, Strand on the Green School
www.strandinfantandnursery.co.uk/Swan-Centre

The Independent School
www.specialneedsuk.org/schooldetails.asp?id=998

Further Reading

Archer, B. and Roberts, P. (1979) 'Design and technological awareness in education.' *Studies in Design Education, Craft and Technology*, 12 (1), 55.

Ball, L., Pollard, E. and Stanley, N. (2010) *Creative Graduates Creative Futures*. London: Creative Graduates Creative Futures Higher Education Partnership and the Institute for Employment Studies.

Edwards, B. (2013) *Drawing on the Right Side of the Brain* (fourth edition). London: Souvenir Press.

Eide, B. and Eide, F. (2011) *The Dyslexic Advantage: Unlocking the Hidden Potential of the Dyslexic Brain*. New York, NY: Hudson Street Press.

Fawcett, A. (ed.) (2001) *Dyslexia: Theory and Good Practice*. London: Whurr Publishers.

Hinshelwood, J. (1917) *Congenital Word Blindness*. London: H.K. Lewis & Company, Ltd.

Isaacs, C. (2019) *Adult Dyslexia: Unleashing Your Limitless Power*. London: Cheryl Isaacs.

Mortimore, T. (2003) *Dyslexia and Learning Style. A Practitioner's Handbook*. London: Whurr Publishers.

Nicolson, R. (2015) *Positive Dyslexia*. Sheffield: Rodin Books.

Nist, S.L. and Kirby, K. (1986) 'Teaching comprehension and study strategies through modeling and thinking aloud.' *Reading Research and Instruction*, 25 (4), 254–264.

Nist, S.L. and Mealey, D.L. (1991) 'Teacher Directed Comprehension Strategies.' In R.F. Flippo and D.C. Caverly (eds) *Teaching Reading and Study Strategies at the College Level* (pp.42–85). Newark, DE: International Reading Association.

Petherbridge, D. (1991) *The Primacy of Drawing: An Artist's View*. London: South Bank Centre.

Power, K. and Iwanczak Forsyth, K. (2018) *The Illustrated Guide to Dyslexia and its Amazing People*. London: Jessica Kingsley Publishers.

Power, K. and Iwanczak Forsyth, K. (2020) *The Bigger Picture Book of Amazing Dyslexics and the Jobs They Do*. London: Jessica Kingsley Publishers.

Pringle Morgan, W. (1896, 7 November) 'A Case of Congenital Word Blindness.' *British Medical Journal*, 2, 1378.

Rankin, Q., Riley, H., Brunswick, N., McManus, C., Chamberlain, R. and Loo, P-W. (2009) 'Inclusive practice: Researching the relationships between dyslexia personality and drawing ability.' In *Proceedings of the INCLUDE 09 Conference*. London: The Royal College of Art. Available at www.rca.ac.uk/research-innovation/research-centres/helen-hamlyn-centre/knowledge_exchange/include-conferences/include-2009/include-2009-proceedings

Redford, J. (dir.) (2012) *The Big Picture: Rethinking Dyslexia*. KPJR Films.

Reid, G. (2016) *Dyslexia: A Practitioner's Handbook*. Oxford: John Wiley & Sons.

Rooke, M. (2016) *Creative, Successful, Dyslexic*. London: Jessica Kingsley Publishers.

Rooke, M. (2018) *Dyslexia is My Superpower (Most of the Time)*. London: Jessica Kingsley Publishers.

Rose, J. (2009) *Identifying and Teaching Children and Young People with Dyslexia and Literacy Difficulties*. Report to the Secretary of State for Children, Schools and Families. Available at: www.thedyslexia-spldtrust.org.uk/media/downloads/inline/the-rose-review.1327396992.pdf

Snowling, M. (2019) *Dyslexia: A Very Short Introduction*. Oxford: Oxford University Press.

Sousa, D.A. (2007) *How the Special Needs Brain Learns*. Volume 1. Thousand Oaks, CA: Corwin Press.

Stein, J. (2010) 'Wobbles, Warbles and Fish – The Brain Basis of Dyslexia.' Magdalen College, Oxford University, UK.

The History of Dyslexia. University of Oxford website: https://dyslexiahistory.web.ox.ac.uk

Vellutino, F. (1979) *Dyslexia: Theory and Research*. Cambridge, MA: MIT Press.

Index

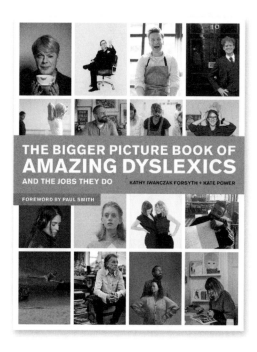

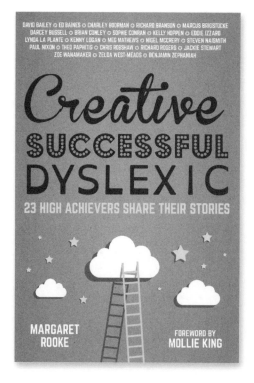

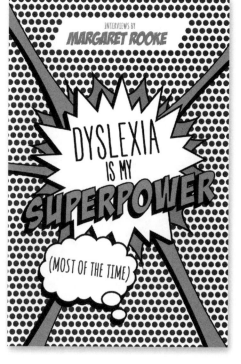